W9-AKS-663

# Breathe the Wind, Drink the Rain

*Notes on Being Alive*

written and illustrated by
## Douglas Wood

*Wind In The Pines Publishing*
*Sartell, Minnesota*

*Dedicated...*

To those who have taken the path to themselves.
To those still looking for it.
And especially...to Bryan and Eric

Illustrations by Douglas Wood
Book design by Jonathan Norberg

Copyright 2002 by Douglas Wood
Second Printing

Published by Wind In The Pines Publishing
3835 Pine Point Road
Sartell, MN 56377
www.douglaswood.com

Distributed by agreement with Adventure Publications, Inc.
820 Cleveland Street South
Cambridge, MN 55008
1-800-678-7006

ISBN: 0-9719971-0-1

Printed in China

*Dear Reader*

This is a little book of advice. Advice on what? I thought you might ask that. Well it began as an answer to a question I've often received on book tours: "How do you get to be a writer?" But as the piece developed, I found it had very little–all right, *nothing*–to do with being a writer, exactly, and a whole lot to do with being a Person. When the time came to title it, however, "How to be a Person" seemed a bit of a far reach (even for an all-knowing wilderness guide).

So, I leave it up to you. If you like this title (as I rather do) leave it. If you can think of a better one, you have my permission to cross this one out and write yours on the cover. In any case, if this small volume helps you or someone you love to smile, or think, or get through a rough patch, or see sunrises or smell honeysuckle, or even become a writer (or postmaster or short-order cook), then I shall be happy indeed.

DW

P.S. Please buy the book before you change the title.

*Wake Up.*

*Notice how things grow.*

*Don't be afraid to*
*see what you see,*
*hear what you hear,*
*think what you think,*
*or feel what you feel.*

*Attend sunrises.*

*Watch turtles.*

*Spend time with what you love.*

*Waste time with whom you love.*

*Save time with...*
*Forget about saving time.*

*Have a favorite chair.*

*Keep your windows clean.*

*Make a great "To Do" list.*
*Do most of it.*

*Sit under big trees.*

*Skinny dip.*

*Learn to brew good coffee,
even if you don't drink it.*

*Smell honeysuckle.*

*Find pussywillows.*

*Be smart.*
*Think of dumb things*
*and do the opposite.*

*Pack light.*

*Leave your own tracks.*

*Travel well,*
*but*
*Be Where You Are Now.*

*Thank everything that's thank-able, everyday.*

*Look often at the moon and stars.*

*Know that The News
is not the world.*

*Accomplish things the way an apple tree accomplishes apples.*

*Taste what you eat*
*and smell what you breathe.*

*Give away.*

*Don't chase butterflies;*

*be still, they'll land on you.*

*Tend your garden.*

*But learn to stop stepping on rakes.*

*Dream.*

*Figure out what you hate about life.*

*Figure out how to love it anyway.*

*Notice how <u>unusual</u> everything is.*

*Make friends with mystery.*

*Set aside Sacred Texts*
*and read the universe.*

*Unwrap the gift of each day.*

*Do the thing you fear.*

*Keep your pilot light lit.*

*Burn old wood,*
  *drink old wine,*
*trust old friends,*
  *and read old books.*

*Get off "Someday I'll" and set sail…*

*For a <u>real</u> island…*
*For a point on the map…*

*For a point in your heart.*

Remember....
    There is only one real question.

And the answer is Yes.